Deep, Dark & Insperational

Vol. 1

Poetry by
James Amdal

Deep, Dark & Insperational
Vol. 1

Poetry by
James Amdal

T&J Publishers

A SMALL INDEPENDENT PUBLISHER WITH A BIG VOICE

Printed in the United States of America by
T&J Publishers (Atlanta, GA.)
www.TandJPublishers.com

© Copyright 2018 by James Amdal

All rights reserved. This book or parts thereof may not be reproduced in any form, stored in a retrieval system, or transmitted in any form by any means-electronic, mechanical, photocopy, recording, or otherwise-without prior written permission of the author, except as provided by United States of America copyright law.

Cover design by James Amdal and Timothy Flemming, Jr. (T&J Publishers)
Book format and layout by Timothy Flemming, Jr. (T&J Publishers)

ISBN: 978-1-7335470-2-4

To contact author, go to:
JamesDAmdal@gmail.com
Facebook: James Amdal

ACKNOWLEDGMENTS

I would like to thank all my family, friends (past, present, and future) love, pain, hurt, and the world around me. All my inspirations, aspirations, and documented emotional experiences and traversals are what guide my creative expressions and output. For all we are confronted with in the path of life which is placed before us; we gain wisdom, strength, happiness and despair. For all goodness to be received, cherished, and stowed away; balance dictates the accompaniment of hardship, pain, sorrow and adversity. The balance for my journey is unfortunately more often tipped towards adversity, pain, and want of unattainable love. I'm not sure, and hopeful, it 'tis not my deemed fated path. But I do persevere and maintain a constant aggressive drive in a forward direction with the best of my ability. I do this by syphoning strength my courage and determination. Though most of my inspiration is derived from raw emotion; I must give much thanks and accreditation to my dear close friends Neyfit Fuentes and Antonio Corral. They are friends for which I love dearly and spent sharing residence with for over 11 years. Just like any friendships, especially when seen and depended on every day, we saw our happy along with our rough and strained times. But through all, we were always there for each other. Though times were not always easy we would not have made it to where we are now without each other. I will forever cherish and value the moments of happiness and accomplishment we were blessed to achieve! I know I previously mentioned my thanks to family. But I should give special thanks to my mother and father whom always gave me great support and stood behind me. Love is want binds us all together and pushes us forward. Without such force we become lost and fall apart. Thank you to all that I have not mentioned which have graced me with true and caring, love and support!

Introduction

I am a very emotionally driven writer. My works span the entire scale for which personal emotional experience encounters and endures. Some works dark while others are joyful. All are mixed with love, pain, happiness and sorrow. Almost every poem I write is deep and usually strikes deep emotional chords with the reader. There are many of my works which provoke deep thought and self-reflection. From this can bring inspiration and understanding of one's self and connection to the world. I am always my own worst and hardest critic but do believe my writing proves worthy of reading and evaluation. I am very happy and proud to share with readers; my words and insight on the world which surrounds us and embodies or souls. I cannot expect all to appreciate; but do thank all those for who I hope will find affection and connection to my direct and raw emotional interruption of our chartering through the world of life. Thank you again to all my readers, fans, inspirations, loves and tutors along the path I have been deemed to follow.

I.

How lonely,
the ticking of a clock,
in an empty room.
Melodic Whispers,
of the passing time
Alone I sit,
all alone it seems
as if, not another soul exists.
Alone I founder,
in an empty ocean
My mind,
the unyielding warden
in a frigid sea
If only for a brief moment,
it seems like eternity
Bathing thyself in sorrows,
that only come forth in silence

The Hourglass

You look into the hourglass
And you see your only past
Watching every grain of sand
You see a helping hand
You see long lost memories
As the wind blows through the trees
Hoping the future will be
Everything that you for see
And then you see it's fate that casts
Everything that's been the past
And now you know that you're just a pawn
While everything is drawn
You continue to walk along
The road on which you belong
And continue on to the end you will
Where the wind remains so still

Unfinished Work

Grinding teeth
surging and pulsing
unstoppable intensity
an unyielding force
Exhilarating and overwhelming
all in parallel instances
Simultaneous observations
in coexisting channels
of interpretation

Unwanted Pain, Unyielding Despair

The world is so cold,
it is so lonely.
The world is bleak
so desperate...
so unholy...
Unwanted fears,
unsanctioned despair.
So near, yet so far...
just beyond reach.
Can you hear me,
see me,
feel me?
I don't think so...
Am I to far . . .
to be near?
So unwanted ...
and unneeded;
it leads me to tears.

I'll dissolve, unknown,
and alone . . .
so silent ... so desperate ...
no road,
leading home.

July, 26 2008

2.

The "Future" follows
no predetermined path . . .
Yet fate does grasp
A strong a hand
upon the wheel of destiny

3.

Unwanted,
unloved
Like a dying flower
Unused and unneeded
only faded and unseen
Once adored
but no more
A castaway for sure
I chase the sun
until it sets
Across the ocean shore

4.

Cold and alone,
In my own fortress of solitude
A prisoner of thy own
entrapping loneliness
Desolate planes
of unending sorrow
Spiked by rare and abrupt
moments of brief
pleasuring relief
Only to be broken back down
by the endless
and unmerciless
Path of life

5.

Feeling up, when I'm down
Feeling happy, when I'm sad
Feeling low, when I'm high
Feeling lost, when I am found
Feel so incomplete,
when you're not around
This roller-coaster of emotion,
is breaking me down
So happy with you
but so lost without
Not sure what to say or do
I just know
that I want you

10/14/2013

6.

Unused minutes
wasted opportunities
The moments of time,
unheeded by the waking eye.

Listless wandering,
mindless comprehension,
In disposed possibilities ..
that comprise the future,
indescribable and ..
distinctly unique.

Unrelenting cravings
for the events that could be;
or not . . .
given the proper equations,
be the bliss of one's
completeness.

And yet;
Indirect is the path that is,
Spontaneously and continuously. . .
placed before them...

Etching into the great canvas,
that is the path of life,
solely unique,
Yet, undeniably interlaced
with all thee comes in contact

Aug 24, 2008

7.

Bipolar is like:
 A roller-coaster
  going through a kaleidoscope

1/16/2015

8.

Thy Morning Sunshine
(Her Gentle Heart)

Good Morning 'Sunshine';
In turn thy brings . . . warmth
and happiness to all thee
disenchanted souls . . .

Thee most endearing souls,
are always the most,
timid and weary.

1/16/2015

A New Day

Today is a new day,
optimistic if one allows.
Heavy thoughts . . . tired mind.
It can lay heavy on one's soul,
if they do allow.
We can really burden ourselves . . .
so unnecessarily at times,
to the point of utter distress.
But always warmth returns
when one allows the sun to rise . . .
Happiness is only self-inficted

July 21, 2008

9.

Is it possible,
to stress the mind so . . .
that the whole world
becomes fuzzy and disconnected . . .
even beyond repair?
Or is it all a,
translucent, trick of the mind?

10.

Drunk as a skunk
High as a kite
I think it's time
for a hit of the pipe

Chillum in one hand
bud in the other
Hoping like heck
I don't spill it all over

With shaky hands
and sweat on my brow
I completed my task
no spillage allowed

II.

Spells of desperation
like an onslaught of needles
and shards of glass
that pierce thy skin
with an unyielding
resilient force of anger
deeper and deeper they tear
Until I scream uncle
into the enveloping emptiness
of despair
Desperation takes hold
as I fght to navigate, my way

Pawing and searching
for the doorway
Scratching and tearing
at the darkness
Screaming through
the tears

Deeply yearning for guidance
A beacon of light
A Shepherd in the night
to guide this lost sheep
Back onto the path
that breathes the warmth
of happiness and delight
A road unseen
and out of reach

12.

Happiness is only temporary
sadness always prevails
It rears it's massive head
like a gargoyle
From the fames of hell
All shall bow to thee
Darkness is the canopy
under which I do dwell

11/19/09

13.

Out of nowhere;
like a punch in the face

A whirlwind, in fury,
an overwhelming force

Rips through my heart,
and through my mind

An emotional upheaval,
with such intensity

A power unmeasured,
as yet before encountered

Not as a hurricane,
filled with destruction and despair

But quite the opposite,
a flood of happiness unmeasured

Of want and yearning,
for who brings the waves

For she is the one;
the force of goodness and happiness

For her I yearn,
for her love and caring

For which in turn
I promise to return

3/21/2016 1:38am

14.

A man needs a woman
like a needle requires thread
Without her
thee is never whole

15.

At frst it's never easy
I would never say that it's so
Bad shit happens
for reasons unknown
Irrational thoughts
followed by even more
Irrational thoughts,
and judgments
Causing irrational, self-,
and mutual destruction
But good always rises above
All the bad that is to be endured
We learn, accept,
and move beyond
All intentional, and unintentional
pain, hurt, and anguish
We must move on
Learn and persevere
Whatever the end game comes to be
To which path is right, will be found
and you will continue on
Just think true
and follow your heart
It's the only way
to see things clearly
Come and do what you do best
Just raise up
and pull yourself together
You know you will always
see this shit through

--

P.S.: Just between you and me
I think this shit, will make it
through the I.C.U.!

2016

16.

Everything lays in fog
from the distance we are standing
Everything is unclear
not like looking in a mirror
Everything falls away
when you're not sure where to stay
Nothing reveals its secrets
on a dark and stormy day

17.

You're crouching in the corner
while the wall is falling down
Your world is a dream
and you don't really care at all
Your mind is unattached
and your voice is unsure
Deep within yourself
you buried your soul

Can you see me?
Can you see me?
I can't see you
I'm too far gone

My vision is distorted
And I can't find my way
Won't you help me through
the world that lies ahead
Everything seems diferent
but I know it is not
Where are you going?
May I follow you?

18.

Trapped six feet under
In a room with no window
nor door
Time no longer has meaning
or relevance

Angela

I think of you often
your beauty beyond compare
The sweetness
from your words and smile
Emanates a brightness
Like the sun
That warms the morning air
Is it fair
that I might meet
one as you
A warm fair soul
enduring and true
I wrote this just for you
Angela

1/17/2017

19.

The sun is coming up
light is creeping through the shades
Another day is waking,
a lazy sun bringing dawn
Though not like any other
a very special day indeed
Another year has passed
the day's meant for celebration
For a sweet young girl
her beautiful name, Ashanti
The time of her birthday
has come around yet again
So let positive vibes rain down
full of happiness and birthday cheer
And best wishes for the new year
And all the many to come

--

To: Ashanti Johnson on her birthday :)
By request and day of: March 27, 2016 Easter Sun
I never do by request; but how could I say no
to this adorable young girl! Happy Birthday, A
I racked my brain all of that day. There finally a couple of lin
Five minutes later, I fulfilled   3/27/2016
my promise to the young girl.
Same day delivery :)

20.

Music shall unite us,
in the light.
And bind us,
in the night.

Peace
Love
Unity
Respect
(Holla' out to all the old
School Kats, party Kids, and Kandy Kids. . . from yonder days.
. . and faded, yet, everlasting memories)

21.

A dead end,
sometimes takes a little backtracking,
A scenic divergence from the path
It sometimes takes
a little scouting ahead
to move forward

22.

I love thy all
thy all unloved

23.

Unbelievable desire
to bring back such glory days of yore
What truly honest
and fun times they were to enjoy
Never can one be the same...
but thy future is not the end

24.

Everyone raise their glass
and cheers to one last good-bye

25.

Life is a strange road, indeed
One moment as I sat
reminiscing while watching "Wheel of Fortune"
and smoking a bowl of fine herb
I realized that,
many of the friends I have today
are all but what's left
of the friends with which
I shared all the amazing times
during, and right after high school
Unbelievable ecstasy flew through my veins
shortly followed by new realizations
That new friends have been added
along the way
Just as true,
and important to me
Comfort and ecstasy intermingled,
and I am immediately filled with
true feelings of contentment
and of wholeness
And of the possibility that
I may have a place in the world
even if only,
my own small part

26.

I drink to get drunk
I get drunk to pass out
I pass out to commit no sins
I commit no sins, to go to heaven
I drink to go to heaven

27.

Money breathes,
good and evil.
Money breeds,
good and evil.
Money needs,
good and evil.
Money is,
good and evil.
Good and evil,
seal the deal.

10/21/2011

28.

It takes saving extra pennies
to acquire extra nickels . . .
But if you spend to many pennies
you end up in a pickle

2/29/2012

29.

"A leg of lamb;
not ham," I say!
Then nodded to Curious Sam
"Or maybe it's Spam"

Inspired by Bob Marley

The sun is shining
and the weather's cold
But keep on shining
to feed my soul
What the day may bring
is still uncertain
And that is fne with me
to watch the day unfold
So sun, keep on shining
it's time to roll
Time to, throw on my shoes
and head out the door
So don't be in denial
and paint on that smile
The world keeps on turning
there's good around the bend
Let the sun keep on shining
shine down on me
Let it keep on shining
Let it keep on shining
Come shine down on me
to break me free
Let me feel whole
and come feed my soul

3-26-2016

31.

Everywhere I go
Everything I see
Reminds me,
of you and me

32.

Everything is a cycle
Everything grows and dies
Everyone lives a lie now
Everyone hears the truth cry

33.

Life is Life
Death is Death
Everything in the middle
is gray
Never black and white
Life is Life
Death is Death
All between is,
our own perception,
our own surreal, reality

34.

Whirlwind of emotion
unsteady happiness
My emotions stand on a pillar
that is lacking foundation
Desperate cries
in depths of darkness
that clouds my mind

Oct. 22 20

35.

Hello, Hello:
Can you hear me breathing?
Do you see my thoughts;
parading in front of you?

36.

I feel so low and down
I feel so tired
I don't know how things
could get much worse than they are
I don't know why
I don't know when
I must have done something
wrong to see the end
How could I know
I should have known
That I would lose again
just like I had before
I loved you more
than I could show
Why did I have to be
so shy in your eyes
Oh can't you see
I do need you
I don't know how to win you
but I'll try again

37.

My bad,
I just dabbed
4:20 y'all

(written on 4/14/2016; in lue of 4/20/2016)

Sub-note from author:

I do not condon nor condeem the intended use of either; pharmecutical, or herbal, pain medications. Nor do I presume to state the benifits and/or side-effects of taking either medication. But, from personal experience, and observation of others) I can say, without a doubt, I have noticed much fewer harmful side-effects and many more benefits from going the herbal path. I have seen much destruction for those who have initially taken pills for an accident, then become addicted and lost everything.

38.

I gaze out at the window sill
gathering snow in the weary cold
the caulk lines that divide the panes
gleam silver, with the moist fresh fakes

They fall in a continuous gentle curtain
blanketing all around with its brilliance
It's gleaming satin white sheen
it covers the mountain tops,
the forests, and the plains
it covers the cities,
and covers the towns

From skyline to roof top
from tree top, to the power line
from car to street sign
from the mail box, to the bird feeder,
of which I can see
through the window in front of which,
I do sit

Thus is the same window
in front of which I do sit

That the fresh new fakes
are continuing to accumulate
So blanket all you see
and all you must
For your beauty is brilliance
to say not, is unjust
Just don't blanket my heart
Do allow the sun,
to continue to shine through my window
To again warm my window sill
And bring warmth back into
this weary heart

4/9/2016

39.

Wisdom can be deafness,
and you can just as easily,
overlook your opponent.

10/1/2011

Long Night

The sun dissolves
 and the sky turns gray
The night is long
 until returns the day

(Sometime during Jr high or high school???)

Soldier of Time

You fight on in the war
Is there nothing more
You don't know where it all began
and how long that you can stand
You hope that you are just as strong
when the next day comes along
You know that you are better than
everything that remains to stand

40.

Nicky, Nicky,
Truly special and unique
There's not another soul in the world
for which one can compare
Of all the girls, I have encountered
Not one, quite like you

You sprang from the shadows
like a tornado, in the night
Upheaval and Chaos
My emotions blown from their nest
As new hatchlings, on unsteady wings
Into first fight, they are cast
Thrust into the turbulence
Falling, then soaring
Disoriented, but energized
Lost while devoted, in search of direction
With an energy unmeasurable
Maybe unknowingly and unintentionally
You filled a great void, and made me whole
When you leave, I ever long for your return
With the emptiness, reasserted
The need of your presence
Is demanded by my heart
Always longing, for the happiness

And craziness, you create inside my head
Knowing, tis always merely temporary
Forever hurting, for you are beyond my reach
And understanding, I could never have you
But always wishing for the chance
To have you all, for myself
I would love you, and care for you
And always, be just and true
Forever there, for understanding
But always giving space
when the time is needed
I would give my life, to protect
so no harm, would ever befall you
To be your knight, in shining armor
Never fearful, and always brave
I would give the world to you
Or as much as I could conquer
For you are worth, every ounce of energy
Every single drop, that can be mustered
To fill your world with eternal happiness
Infinite contentment, and joy
Forever yearning, for the chance and opportunity
For you to be, the one and only
That I could cherish, for my own

To relish, in true blissfulness
Throughout the eternity of our time

April - May 2017

41.

That's all life is...
 About being creative
Just hope you paint a nice portrait
 when it's over!

42.

Cherish the day. . .
For there are never
any guarantees
for another to follow

--

8/15/2017
Dedicated to My Aunt Denise who passed away the evening before. She shall be greatly missed by all

43.

Just when I had told myself
There is not a girl for me
Slipped into my life you quite did
With an unseen stealth
Your sweetness, and loveliness
And endearing true soul
I fell in love; charmed on the spot
By your warmth and caring
"Twas quite taken into
But a battle has just been waged
An internal struggle, per say
My subconscious, self protection program
Always ready and waiting
Poised for the sneak-attack
Throwing obstacles and detrimental behavior
In front of my conscious mind's borders
All in great fury, and dedication
Driven by its vowed protection
for the wall around my heart
Though only hurt but a few times
The pains inflicted
Were grave and scarring
And penetrated rather deeply
So up came the wall
Allow no one else in

Thy subconscious infantry
Is grand and mighty
And very quick on the draw
But my conscious mind is valiant
Dedicated and skillful
And beyond qualified
In winning the battle for you
So I do pray
For your understanding
And enough time
To acquire my nerve
And win the battle
For you and your love
I much do need and desire
Or at least a chance
To make a go
For thy never knows
You could be the one
For which I was meant
To wait for. .

Oct 10 2017

44.

The Dream . . .
of the knowledge of the Elders.

To seek . . .
out the light of the future.

Conquest on the road . . .
. . . to learn the truth,
of self-being.

Nov. 18, 2006

Ashanti

There's this sweet little girl,
who writes me poems
What a great honor, I do feel
to receive such gifts
carefully, skillfully, and handcrafted
just for me.
So, here I shall go again
Must, dutifully and honorably, return the favor
I'll dive right in, with pure devotion
Try and scratch something out
With a tired mind, but without any doubt
I'll come up with a work
Not sure if, good or bad
But words will fill the page
Regardless, of the outcome
I'm sure she will appreciate
Either way, for sure
Though I must figure out something soon
Before my head, marries thy pillow
My mind is getting rather foggy
And eyelids rather droopy
And hasten to work my craft
Before my brain becomes detached
And has vacated the realm of reality
Ashanti writes me poems
And is beautiful and fair
Not like the ugly ones
In the place, down past the stairs
She is a very caring person
and polite to be sure

But she is always clever, and full of wit
and as such, can be quite a little shit
For, Ashanti is one cool cat
Who all must adore
To go without her presence
Life would be such a bore
So I do believe I did it
Composed for her, another poem
I hope she does like it
I'll fnd out soon enough
Time to snuggle up in my bed
it's getting kind of late
Tomorrow morning is coming
Way too soon, it seems
So off to sleep I go
To everyone out there listening
I bid you sweet dreams

April 17, 2016 2:37am

45.

Feeling all alone
You stand in the cold
Not knowing
Where you belong
You talk to the people
Who walk from the walls,
unaffected, at all
By the sudden loss of time
You lose distinction
And begin to fade, into the dark
Walk away, re-establish direction
But don't leave your cause behind

46.

One can only
receive help if
they ask for help.

But by asking . . .
They must also
Only be willing and ready
To accept it
Then enact it
and utilize it,
Together

47.

Hey everybody
Can you see me
Hey everyone
Come see me
I am all alone here
And I can't break free

Uncertain Paths

Distant voices
Distant calls
Withered images
Within the walls
Parted mind
Parted Soul
Furthered time
Uncertain cold
Watching you
I see myself
We're not the same
For we have changed
For better things
We want the same

Stray Thought

The stray thought blew through
uncertainly again you see
like a melody

Beneath The Shadows

Beneath the Shadows
You will hide the worst of times
like a dark cellar

The Rain

Watch the rain fall to the ground
Does not ever make a sound
If things could be so simple and free
I would understand all but you and me

Empty Road

To walk along the road
All alone in the night
Brings about two opposites
One feeling of peace
And one feeling of loneliness

Lost

Lost in time
With no direction
Feeling all alone
But not misunderstood
You grasp for words
But none shall come
Lost in love with
One Lost in emotion

Rain

Rain
Moist, renewing
Essence of Spring
Something more than water
Escape

Grass

Grass
Green, soft
Returning in Spring
A nuisance for all
Everlasting

48.

I'm lost
Not in where I'm at
Not in where I'm going to
Not like a stranger along an untraveled highway
But just lost in emotion
Unsure of what to do
Unsure of where to go
Unsure of all that's you

I'm alone
Not without friends
Not without enemies
Not like an oasis in the middle of a desert
But with no one to be with
With no one to talk to
With no one to laugh with
With no one to care for

I'm confused
Not with the weather
Not with the alarm clock
Not like a fish out of water
But confused about you
Confused about me
Confused about all
Not all that you see

49.

Pick up the phone
There is no destination
Who will you know
This is your creation
There are no limits
For what you can see
Hold on just a minute
Pass on with me

Peer out the door
There is the war
In your mind
There is no more
Words come in silence
Your misery is time
Look and find
The un-fined line

50.

Swirling, merging, devouring
A variable, never ending and ever changing maze
A fiery, clashing; and inter-looping
Collage of colors and emotions
Like an eternal pin wheel of pulsing
And sporadic pitching, weaving, and cycling
A volatile mix of speed and direction
My mind is frantic
full of mixed, good and wonderful;
Yet intimidating and exhilarating
Interweaving collection of thoughts and consciousnesses
I cling desperately, yet confidently
with fevered and bruised
Cracked, shaking, white knuckled hands
Exhausted, yet contained and controlled
I grasp upon my life vehicle's
wheel of direction and elevation
Clinging in desperation to thy path
of salvation and redemption
Through squinted, tired and red-veined eyes
To persevere along the challenging and forked
Road of struggle and success
Always watchful and weary
Of the upcoming obstacles and hurdles
Intermittently and often blindly
Selecting and detouring with uncertain confdence
On the paths laid before me
Always hoping for normal and routine
Filled with happiness and contentment
But ever mindfully watching

For divergences into sorrow and pain
Yet, always valiantly weathering and maintaining
At least a mediocre piloting
Of thy journey and adventure
An ever changing and unseen race
To the unseen convergence of present into future
A course of thy chosen direction
Yet, inevitably and always fatedly cast
An unseen traversal
From point of origin to destination
With frayed, though, resilient nerves
I pilot my vehicle of fortune and pain
Not always joyful and fulfilling
Yet always beyond one's complete control
Curtained with varied and vague
Degrees of understanding
Ever abundant and enduring
A see-sawed balance of wants and needs
Perceived as chosen
But always dictated by time

12/19/2017

51.

Melancholy strikes me
Like an unsettling disease
Clad in cracked and tear stained cheeks
With year weathered and long since drought-stricken eyes
I bear the scars of a learned man
One wise from enduring, long scores
of victory and defeat
Catapulting over ever more challenging hurdles
A treacherous traversal along the road of trials
Some paths are coursed and guided
With simplicity and ease
Drawn from ingrained and familiar repetition
Others blindly plotted and tested
with confidence in one's, self hurdling
into the unknown
Confidence, totally and wholly, procured from faith
Faith graced upon them by true love
Hastened only by mutual self doubt
But explored, expanded, and grown
Through an eternally, bonded and trusted, union of love
Only in unison, can thy both endure
With coupling brings strength and protection
Unyieldingly devoted assurance and direction
When binded by soul and heart
All challenges and quests thus presented
Will be courageously and valiantly approached
Joined together we can achieve in conquest
Embracing all gained and won happiness
Siphoning from within
A vast and abundant well of strength

Fortifed and reinforced
By trust and loyalty to each other
Without such love
Life's quest becomes in surmountable
Darkness and emptiness will enshroud us
Like a dank and heavy fog
Obscuring all hope and sight of the path
Only held together by love
Can we fnd our beacon of light
Piercing and scorching the darkness
It's brilliance radiating from our
metaphorical lighthouse
Hand in hand we walk together
Faithfully and fatedly gliding into the future

2/11/2018

52.

Lost in, but without true love
Unwanted, and without regard
Cast into a terrible and unforgiving sea
Hopelessly clinging to a fatedly, failing crusade
To keep my weak and exhausted soul
Above the cold, draining, and frigid waters
Drowning yet desperately grasping
Grasping and searching
For an unseen and unreachable
Life preserver of hope
Bestowing the essential saving grace
Every attempt to plot and course
The impassable channel of love
I am always blindly overtaken
And viciously swept overboard
Into a whirlpool of incomprehensible pain and sufering
Barely living and recycling
Until redemption day releases my bindings
Tethered to my course of pain
Always knowing; yet not knowing, and knowing
That my blind faith is destined
To overcome all and valiantly reach
Deliverance from my sorrow and stormy passage
Brilliance and happiness as my shepherd
Dreamily sailing into my appointed safe harbor

2/22/2018

53.

Oh, how I wish the stars were mine
to give them all to you
There to build up all of your
hopes and dreams
I'd share the whole world
with you

6/2/2018

54.

The sun rises and shines
upon the new day
Yesterday's sorrows and troubles
vanquished and put to rest
With new found hope and enthusiasm
the new trials and challenges before us
must be afronted with newly found
strength, courage, and self-inficted confidence
Life marches on, with, or without us
Unyieldingly, progressing ever forward
It is upon us wholly
to test and push ourselves
Beyond our known boundaries and strengths
Ceaselessly learning, new, and improving upon
Our prior gained abilities at conquest and victory
Celebrating and rejoicing our accomplishments
with those dearest and closest to us
Only in partnership and union
Can we attain our highest set goals
Alone, one's greatest strengths can fail
against the unseen hardships and weariness
That comes before relief and happiness
Life's journey can be painful and burdening
But all struggles can be overcome
with the bondage of true love
There will never be defeat

55.

To the wobble of the fan
Mesmerized by the constant spinning, of my mind
Desperate cries for stabilization
And frail hopes that it is even a possibility
Always anxious and fearful of change
But truly knowing this cannot go on
I dry my eyes, and lift myself up
With uncertain timidness and blanketed eyes
I raise my head while my mind screams in pain
While vainly grasping, for warm helping hands
Always just out of sight and beyond my reach
My head aches in pain
Confned by an infnite fortress of solitude
Sentenced to eternal loneliness and despair
Life imprisonment, by the self-made wall
That has seemingly, forever surrounded
And guarded my hurt and scarred heart
Love sick over a true and endearing soul
One so perfect, yet forever beyond my reach
For I know I could never have her
And I acknowledge she does not need me
In the same way as I do need her
But just to at least have her friendship
And warming rays of sunshine in my life
I must settle for what I am given
To treasure her friendship
And accept my place, I must
Bury thy feelings deep within my heart
And try to carry forward, I try
Destiny and fate has laid my path
And mine is deemed a solo journey

Some of us must travel alone
Through the journey on life's highway
And I am one of those
Courted to my fate and journey
Maybe there is some grand task
Waiting on the road ahead
One that requires only one soul
To be sacrificed for the insurance of balance
For those earmarked for happiness
There must be those to carry on alone
Their destination already predetermined
But unknown and unseen
Until their future merges with their present
I accept my role, for we are all pawns
In a much grander game
Beyond one soul's comprehension

56.

It is a time of darkness and confusion
Desperately clinging to frail sanity
Overcome with uncontrolled and overwhelming
Feelings and emotions derived from love
Love for one so true
But the possibility of attaining
Uncertain and yet out of reach
The thoughts of being without
Her complete and true presence in my life
Voids and empties my soul
But to envision such a union
Also inflicts pain and hurt
For such a union would in turn
Scar and hurt another soul
For which I deeply loved and cared for
Thy situation causes deep internal confliction
Thus the foreseeable answer and conclusion
Is blinded and invisible to thy eyes
Only fate will determine the end and the beginning
For all that has occurred, pain and happiness
Will only be together, converged and endured
Life always leads us to conquer our trials
Prevailing through pain to achieve true happiness
Mistakes only lead to knowledge and strength
Failing does not always lead to defeat
Understanding one's true path and desires
Will only lead to strength and confidence
Falling into despair and loneliness
Can only bury and obliterate thy dreams
How can I move forward alone on thy path

Unforeseeably placed before me
An unexpected, seemingly, overpowering hurtle
Like an un-bridged gap in the road of life
With no possible way to backtrack or detour
Only possible to overtake with union and partnership
Lacking such a bond, all thy strength
Seems to be draining into the gap
Pulling me forward into the emptiness
Is this the end or is my destiny
Still to achieve wholeness and victory
Over all hurt and incompleteness
I hope the end is only the beginning
But my eyes are blinded and incapable
Of knowing thy true outcome.
Please let me accomplish and move forward
And not fall into the nothingness
I pray that darkness and sorrow
Do not prevail and dictate my future
Is happiness only a dream for me
Or will fate pave a path for me to my dreams
My dreams to be a father and a protector
A true and ever-loving soul-mate
To one dear and faithful
Is that a dream beyond my deserved fate
Can I make it in achieving my hopes and dreams
Or am I destined to always be slated
To only dream of such fulfilling desires
I can only live by clinging to the possibility
Of thy dreams becoming my destined reality

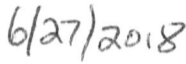

6/27/2018

57.

Sinking into solitude
I deeply, inwardly ponder
While dreaming of wholeness
and of completion in harmony
Aspirations and yearning
For the opportunity and my chance
To create a family of my own
For which to cherish and love
I'd give undying devotion and care
to bring a new life and soul
Into the world that surrounds us
Teaching, while learning thyselves
Relishing and absorbing all happiness and pain
That shall be blessed upon us
Forever resilient and persevering
For such a task and responsibility
It is the gift that life bestows
And must be our true intended purpose
For us to bear and carry out

About The Author

James Amdal was born in Saint Louis, Missouri. He came into this world at Missouri Baptist Hospital on December 22, 1980. He and his parents moved when he was young to Roodhouse, then Jacksonville, IL. James then attended grade school, middle school, and high school in Jacksonville.

James' mother's family came from Saint Louis, and hia father's family originated from Chicago. In 2006, James moved backed to South City, Saint Louis, where his parents met. In mid 2007, he moved to Collinsville, IL. To this day, James remain a working class man residing in the Saint Louis area.

This book not only contains James' creative poetic work, but his photography. James is a self taught, fully manual/film camera, photographer and musician. He love the arts and desires to spread love, wisdom, inspiration and self-exploration.

To contact author, go to:
JamesDAmdal@gmail.com
Facebook: James Amdal

www.ingramcontent.com/pod-product-compliance
Lightning Source LLC
Chambersburg PA
CBHW030331080526
44584CB00012B/807